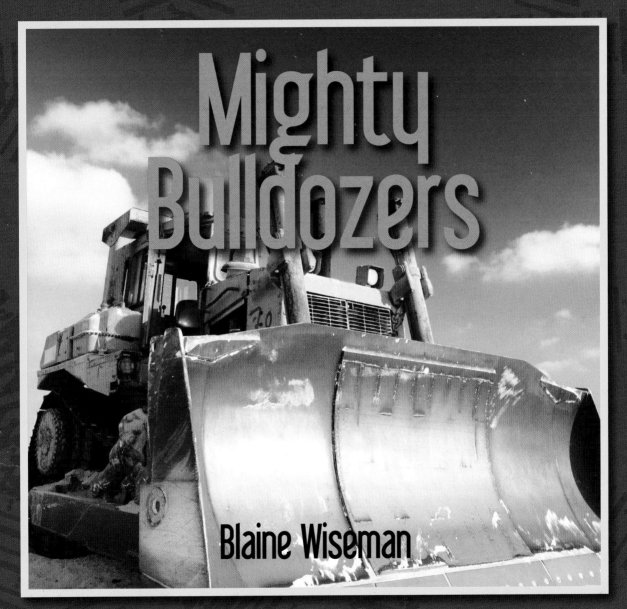

Mighty Bulldozers

Blaine Wiseman

WEIGL PUBLISHERS INC.
"Creating Inspired Learning"
www.weigl.com

Published by Weigl Publishers Inc.
350 5th Avenue, 59th Floor
New York, NY 10118
Website: www.weigl.com

Library of Congress Cataloging-in-Publication Data available upon request.
Fax 1-866-44-WEIGL for the attention of the Publishing Records department.

ISBN 978-1-61690-142-4 (hard cover)
ISBN 978-1-61690-143-1 (soft cover)

Printed in the United States of America in North Mankato, Minnesota
1 2 3 4 5 6 7 8 9 0 14 13 12 11 10

052010
WEP264000

Editor: Heather C. Hudak
Design: Terry Paulhus

All of the Internet URLs given in the book were valid at the time of publication. However, due to the dynamic nature of the Internet, some addresses may have changed, or sites may have ceased to exist since publication. While the author and publisher regret any inconvenience this may cause readers, no responsibility for any such changes can be accepted by either the author or the publisher.

Every reasonable effort has been made to trace ownership and to obtain permission to reprint copyright material. The publishers would be pleased to have any errors or omissions brought to their attention so that they may be corrected in subsequent printings.

Weigl acknowledges Getty Images as its primary image supplier for this title.

CONTENTS

What are Bulldozers?

Have you ever wondered how construction workers move huge piles of dirt and tear down buildings? They use big machines, such as bulldozers. A bulldozer can be used to fill holes, flatten ground, or move heavy objects.

Bulldozers have a large blade on the front. The blade pushes dirt from place to place. Some bulldozers have a hook on the back. The hook is used to rip up the ground.

Bulldozers are named after bulls. Like bulls, bulldozers are very strong.

Big Bulls

How big is your family car? The average car weighs about 4,000 pounds (1,814 kilograms). Even the smallest bulldozers weigh twice as much as a car.

The world's biggest bulldozer weighs more than 22 elephants. It is 16 feet (4.9 meters) tall, 41 feet (12.5 m) long, and 24 feet (7.3 m) wide. This big machine has enough power to move 485,000 pounds (219,992 kg) at one time.

Moving Materials

Did you know that a bulldozer can move 20,000 pounds (9,072 kg) in seconds? It would take about 200 people to push the same amount of rock by hand.

Bulldozers can move almost any object. They can rip apart mountains and push rocks and dirt to a new place. The huge blade on the front of a bulldozer pushes dirt, rocks, trees, and other objects.

Making Tracks

Why are some bulldozers called crawlers or caterpillars? These bulldozers have tracks instead of wheels. The tracks make the bulldozer look like a caterpillar crawling along the ground.

Tracks keep bulldozers from sinking on wet, muddy, or sandy ground. They move more easily than wheels across uneven ground. Bulldozers on tracks need less space to turn. This makes working in tight spaces easier.

Rip It Up

Have you ever used your fingers like a hook to dig in mud or sand? The hook on a bulldozer is called a ripper. It is a powerful claw. It digs into the ground and tears it apart.

Bulldozers can have many rippers that are side-by-side on the back of the machine. Work can be done faster if more than one ripper is used.

Some rippers are so strong that they can break through hardened **lava**.

Bull Blades

Did you know that bulldozers have more than one type of blade? Bulldozers have three main types of blades. Each does a different job.

The straight blade is short and flat. It is used to loosen and level dirt. The second type of blade is tall and curved. It has side wings to keep objects in place. This type of blade is used to gather and move materials. A third type of blade is used to push rocks and other objects. It has smaller sides and is less curved than the other types of blades.

Army Armor

How can bulldozers be used to help soldiers? Trash, damaged cars, or other items sometimes block roads where soldiers work. Bulldozers that are covered in armor push these items out of the way. They also protect soldiers from bullets, **land mines**, and **grenades**.

Bull Rider

How do drivers move the giant parts of a bulldozer? The driver controls the bulldozer using levers. One lever changes the direction and speed of the bulldozer. A second lever moves the blade up and down.

A special system is used to power the blade and the ripper. This system makes large amounts of energy by squeezing oil from one tube to another. This creates power in a part of the bulldozer that had none before. Oil flows into a tube when a lever is pushed. This makes the blade or ripper move.

19

Bringing Down the House

Have you ever seen a house being torn down? Sometimes, people want to tear down an old house to build a new one on the land. A bulldozer can knock down the old house in just a few minutes. Then, the machine can be used to clear the pieces away.

Bulldozers also can be used to move around waste. At **landfills**, bulldozers push garbage into holes. Then, these big machines cover the holes with dirt.

21

Build a Bulldozer

Supplies
tape, scissors, ruler, pipe cleaner, colored
pencils or crayons, three toilet paper tubes,
glue, black and yellow construction paper,
and a small, rectangular box

1. With the help of an adult,
   measure each side of the box
   with the ruler. Cut the yellow
   construction paper to size.

2. Glue the yellow construction
   paper to each side of the box.
   Make sure the box is completely
   covered. The yellow box will
   be the main part of the
   bulldozer's body.

3. Using the colored pencils or
   crayons, draw windows, doors,
   lights, and other designs on the
   outside of the box.

4. Cut the toilet paper tube in half
   lengthwise, and spread it apart.
   This is the bulldozer blade.

5. Bend the pipe cleaner, and
   tape it to the back of the toilet
   paper tube.

6. Tape the two ends of the
   pipe cleaner to the front
   of the bulldozer.

7. Cut two pieces of black
   construction paper twice
   as long as the bulldozer.

8. Fold one piece of construction
   paper in half, and tape the two
   ends together. This is one of the
   tracks. Do the same with the
   other piece of black
   construction paper.

9. Tape the tracks to each side
   of the bulldozer. Place a toilet
   paper tube inside each track
   to hold it open.

10. Have fun using the bulldozer to
    push around blocks and toys.

Find Out More

To learn more about bulldozers, visit these websites.

Bulldozer Video
http://video.yahoo.com/watch/772344/3300420

Great Bulldozer
www.squidoo.com/bulldozers

Everything About Construction
www.kenkenkikki.jp/special/no02/e_index.htm

Glossary

grenades: explosive devices

landfills: places where people in a city or town take their trash

land mines: bombs that are planted in the ground and explode when weight is applied to them

lava: hot liquid rock that flows from a volcano

Index